Jupiter

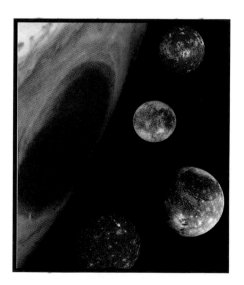

by
Christine Taylor-Butler

Children's Press
An Imprint of Scholastic Inc.
New York Toronto London Auckland Sydney
Mexico City New Delhi Hong Kong
Danbury, Connecticut

These content vocabulary word
builders are for grades 1–2.

Consultant: Michelle Yehling, Astronomy Education Consultant

Photo Credits:

Photographs © 2008: Finley Holiday Films: cover, 2, 4 bottom left, 7, 23; Holiday Film Corp.: 5 bottom right, 13; NASA: back cover, 1, 4 top, 5 top left, 5 top right, 5 bottom left, 9, 15, 17, 19; Photo Researchers, NY/Detlev van Ravenswaay: 4 bottom right, 11; PhotoDisc/Getty Images via SODA: 23 spot art.

Illustration Credit:

Illustration pages 20–21 by Greg Harris.

Book Design: Simonsays Design!
Book Production: The Design Lab

Library of Congress Cataloging-in-Publication Data
Taylor-Butler, Christine.
Jupiter / by Christine Taylor-Butler.—Updated ed.
    p. cm.—(Scholastic news nonfiction readers)
Includes bibliographical references and index.
ISBN-13: 978-0-531-14696-5 (lib. bdg.)   978-0-531-14761-0 (pbk.)
ISBN-10: 0-531-14696-0 (lib. bdg.)   0-531-14761-4 (pbk.)
1. Jupiter (Planet)—Juvenile literature. I. Title.
QB661.T39 2007
523.45—dc22   2006102768

ER 523.45 Tay

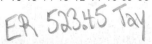

CONTENTS

WORD HUNT

Look for these words as you read. They will be in **bold**.

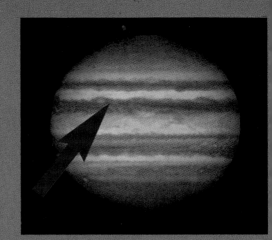

bands
(bandz)

Jupiter
(**joo**-pih-tuhr)

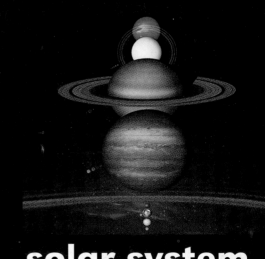

solar system
(**soh**-lur **siss**-tuhm)

4

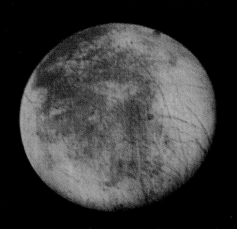

Europa
(yur-**oh**-pah)

Io
(**eye**-oh)

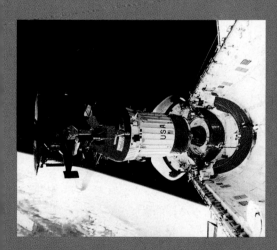

space probe
(spayss prohb)

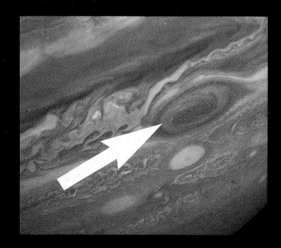

storm
(storm)

5

Jupiter!

Can you dance on **Jupiter**?

No. You cannot dance on Jupiter.

You cannot even stand on the planet.

Jupiter is made mostly of liquid and gas.

There are lots of clouds on Jupiter.

They make the planet look like it has stripes.

The clouds form **bands** of color. They are blue, brown, yellow, white, and red.

The bands move in opposite directions.

The wind in the bands blows very fast.

On Jupiter, winds have blown as fast as 400 miles (644 kilometers) per hour.

Jupiter is the fifth planet from the Sun.

It is the largest planet in the **solar system**.

You could fit more than 1,300 Earths inside Jupiter.

Jupiter

Earth

Sun

11

On Jupiter, there is a **storm** called the Great Red Spot.

This storm is two times wider than our whole planet.

This storm is like a hurricane on Earth. But it has lasted at least 340 years.

It is one of Jupiter's many storms.

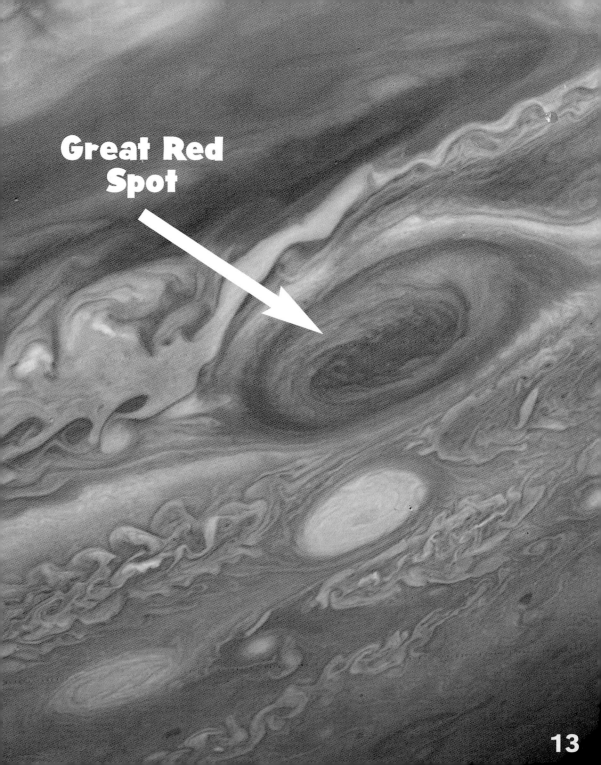

Great Red
Spot

Jupiter has more moons than any other planet.

It has at least 63 moons.

One of Jupiter's largest moons is **Io** (**eye**-oh).

Io has many volcanoes.

A volcano is a mountain made of lava. Lava is hot melted rock or melted rock that has cooled and hardened.

Io is about the same size as Earth's moon.

Europa is another of Jupiter's largest moons.

This moon looks very different from Io.

It is covered with ice.

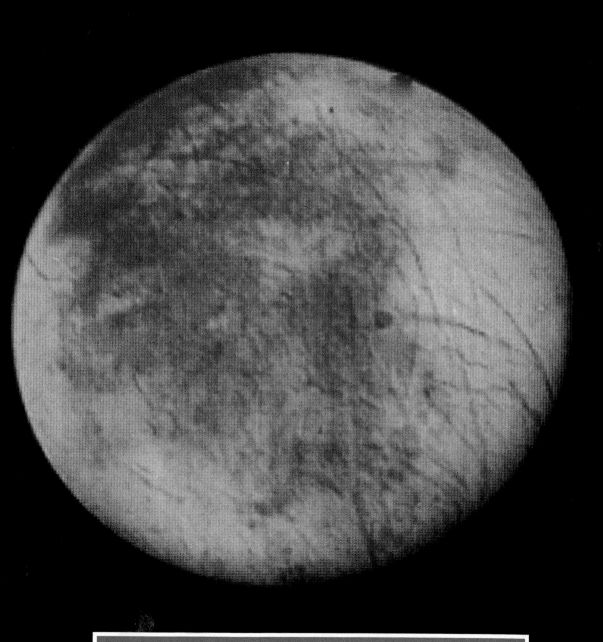

The layer of ice on Europa's surface is several miles thick.

The **space probe** *Galileo* went to Jupiter.

For almost eight years, it helped scientists learn about Jupiter's storms and moons.

In 2003 *Galileo* could do no more.

Scientists at NASA crashed it into Jupiter. They did not want it to hit any of Jupiter's moons.

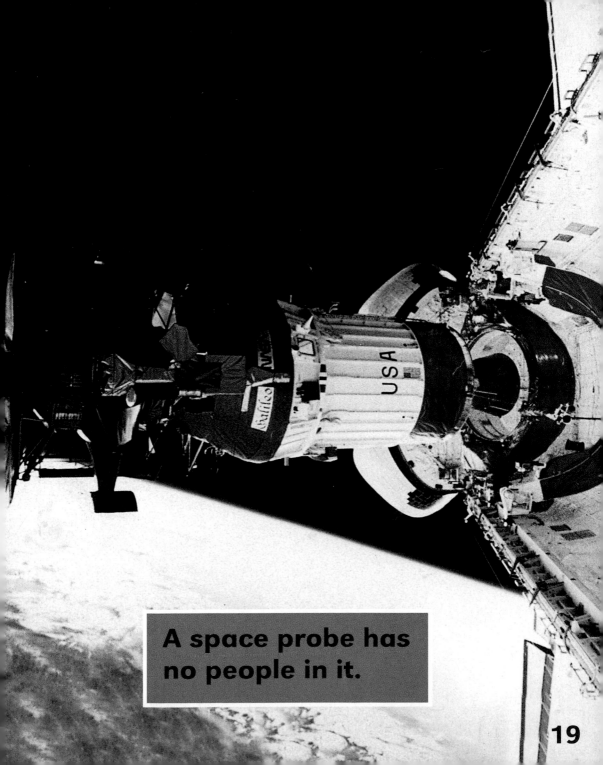

A space probe has no people in it.

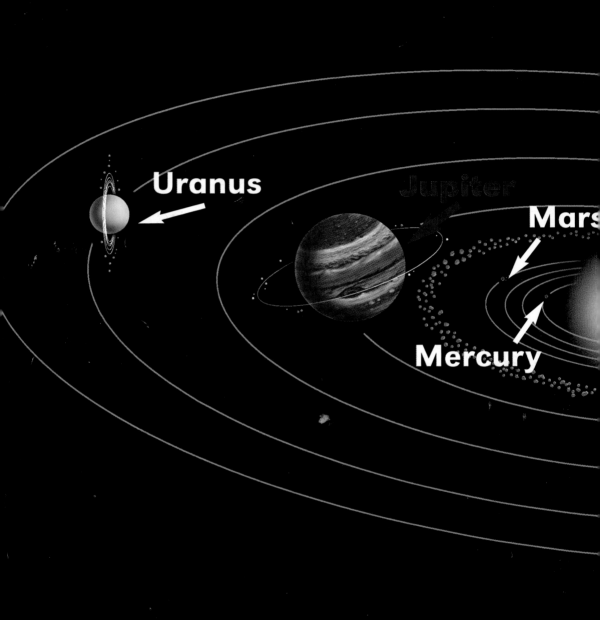

Uranus

Jupiter

Mars

Mercury

JUPITER
IN OUR SOLAR SYSTEM

Sun

Venus

Saturn

Earth

Neptune

YOUR NEW WORDS

bands (bandz) long strips of clouds

Europa (yur-**oh**-pah) one of Jupiter's largest moons

Io (**eye**-oh) one of Jupiter's largest moons

Jupiter (**joo**-pih-tuhr) a planet named after the king of the Roman gods

solar system (**soh**-lur **siss**-tuhm) the group of planets, moons, and other things that travel around the Sun

space probe (spayss prohb) a vehicle with robotic equipment used to explore space

storm (storm) violent weather with strong winds

Earth and Jupiter

A year is how long it takes a planet to go around the Sun.

 **1 Earth year
=365 days**

 **1 Jupiter year
=4,331 Earth days**

A day is how long it takes a planet to turn one time.

 **1 Earth day
= 24 hours**

 **1 Jupiter day
= 10 Earth hours**

A moon is an object that circles a planet.

 **Earth has
1 moon.**

 **Jupiter has 63
moons with more
being found all
the time.**

**Jupiter is the fastest
turning planet in our
solar system.**

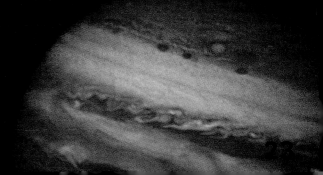

INDEX

FIND OUT MORE
Book:
Burnham, Robert. *Children's Atlas of the Universe.* Pleasantville, NY:
Reader's Digest Children's Publishing, Inc., 2000.

Web site:
Solar System Exploration
http://sse.jpl.nasa.gov/planets

MEET THE AUTHOR
Christine Taylor-Butler is the author of more than twen-
ty books for children. She holds a degree in Engineering
from M.I.T. She lives in Kansas City with her family, where
they have a telescope for searching the skies.